Coney Island during the pandemic. The deserted boardwalk, with its motionless rides and wild faces. On the beach, people living in tents. The eternal ocean.

The Pier

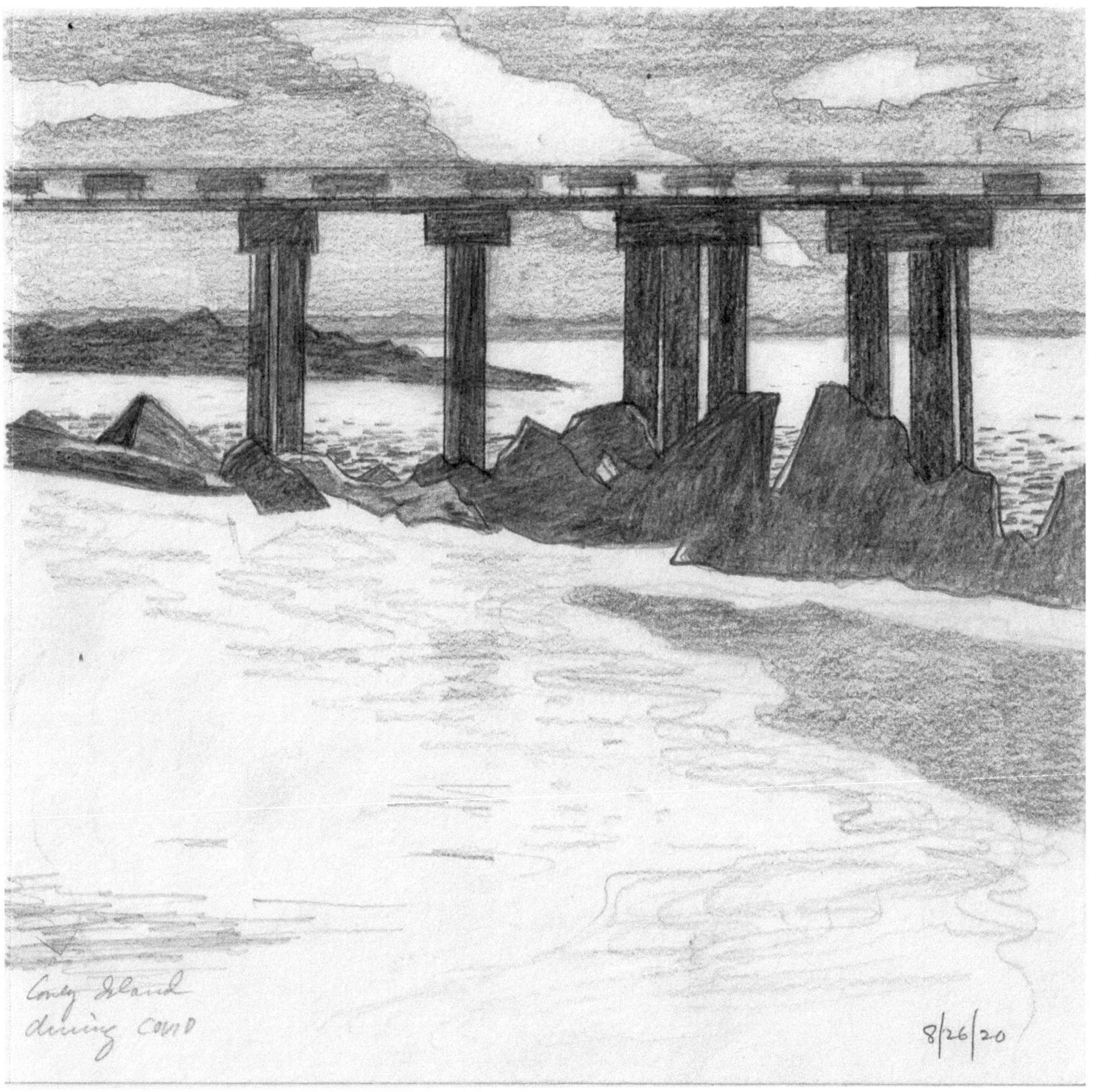

Coney Island
during COVID
8/26/20

Woman Selling Masks

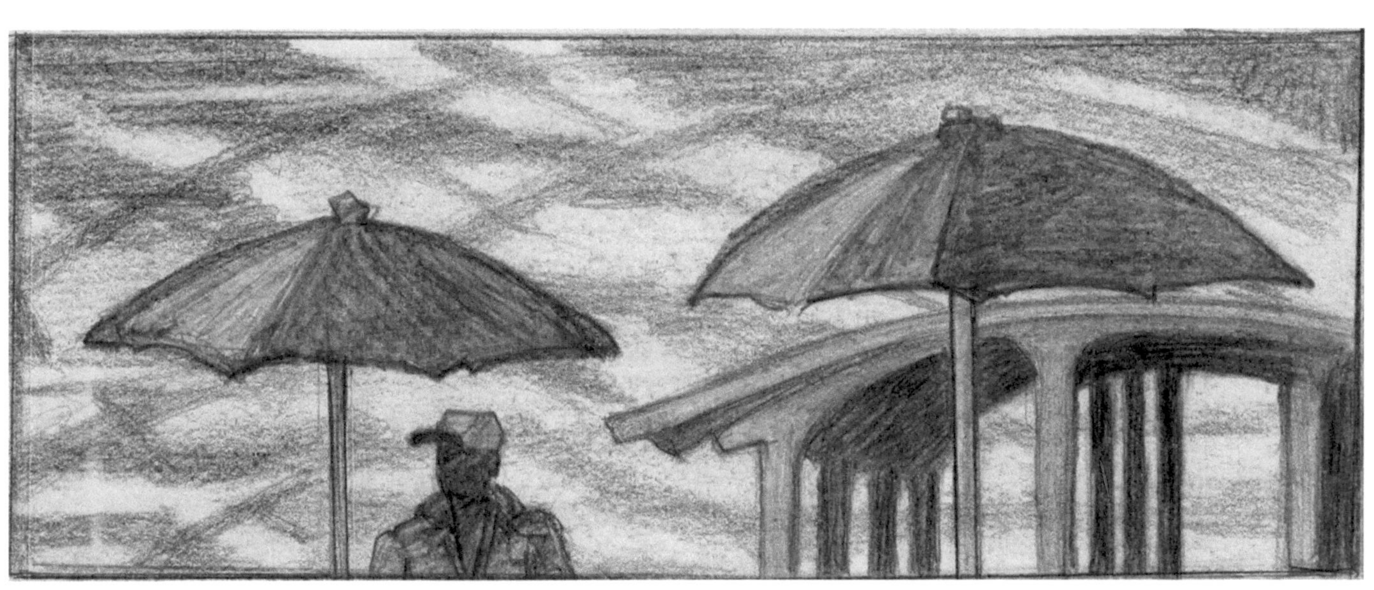

Lifeguard and Tent

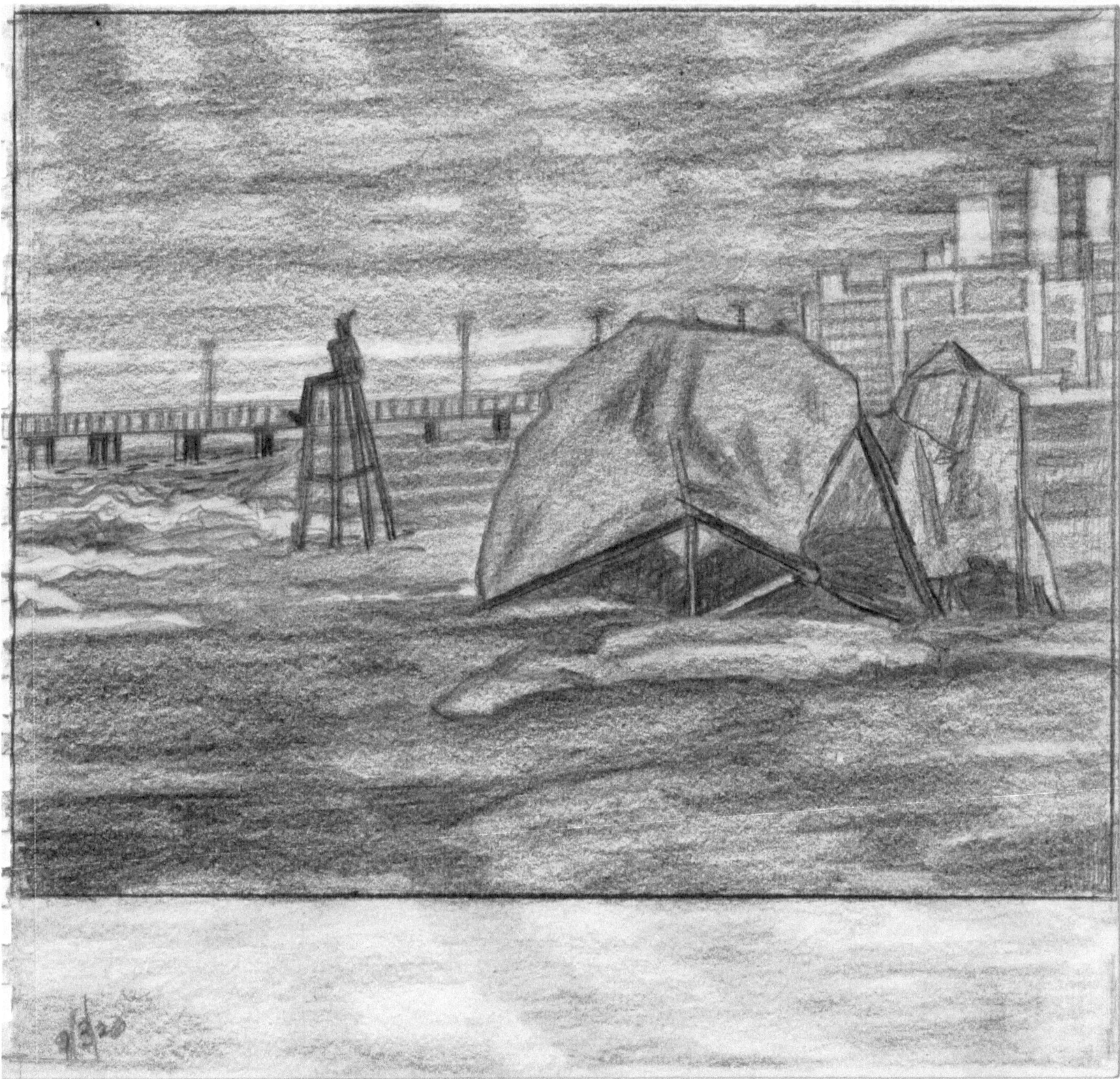

Coney Island Faces

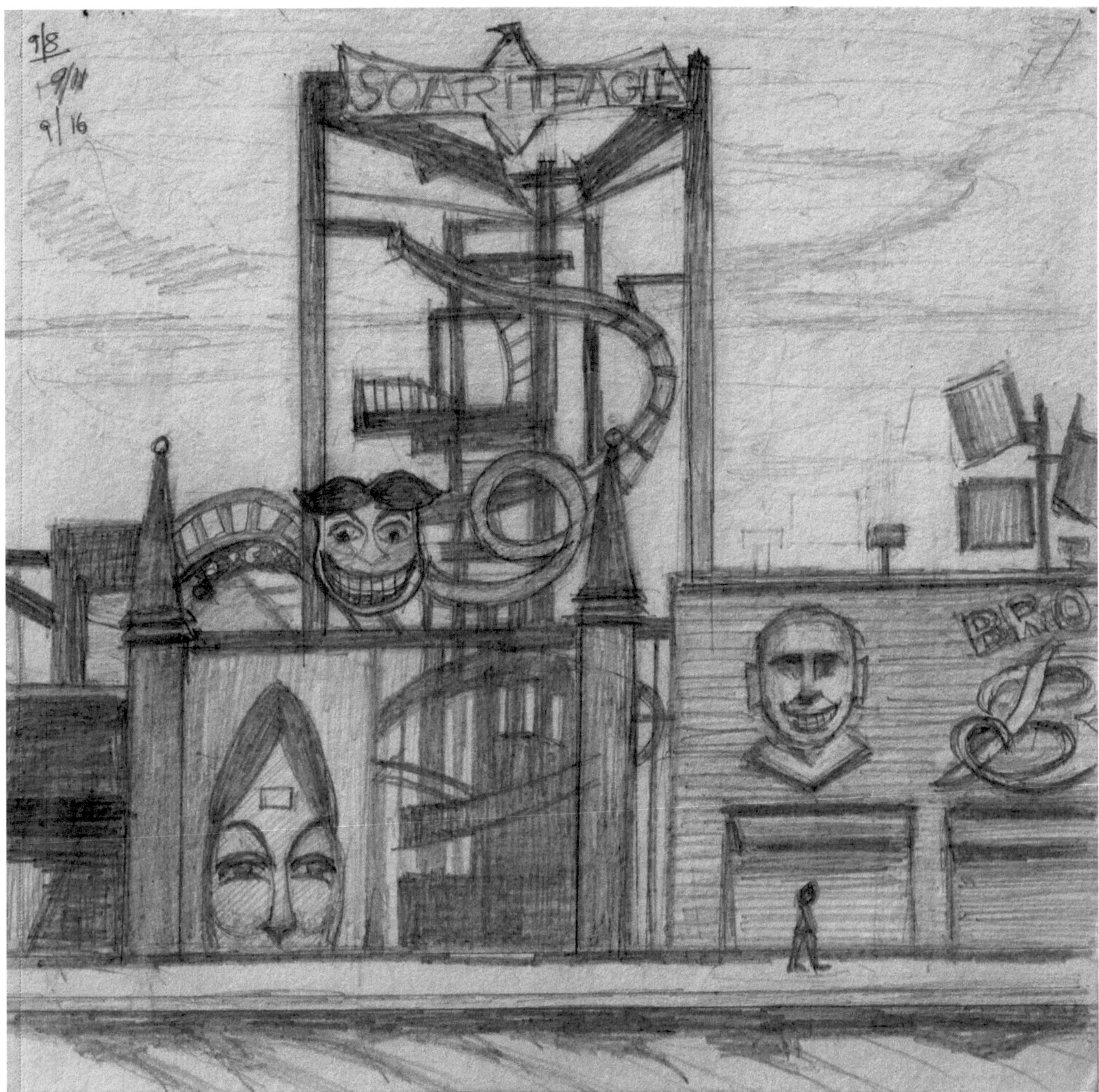
9/8
9/11
9/16
SOAR THE EAGLE
BRO

Woman and Arches

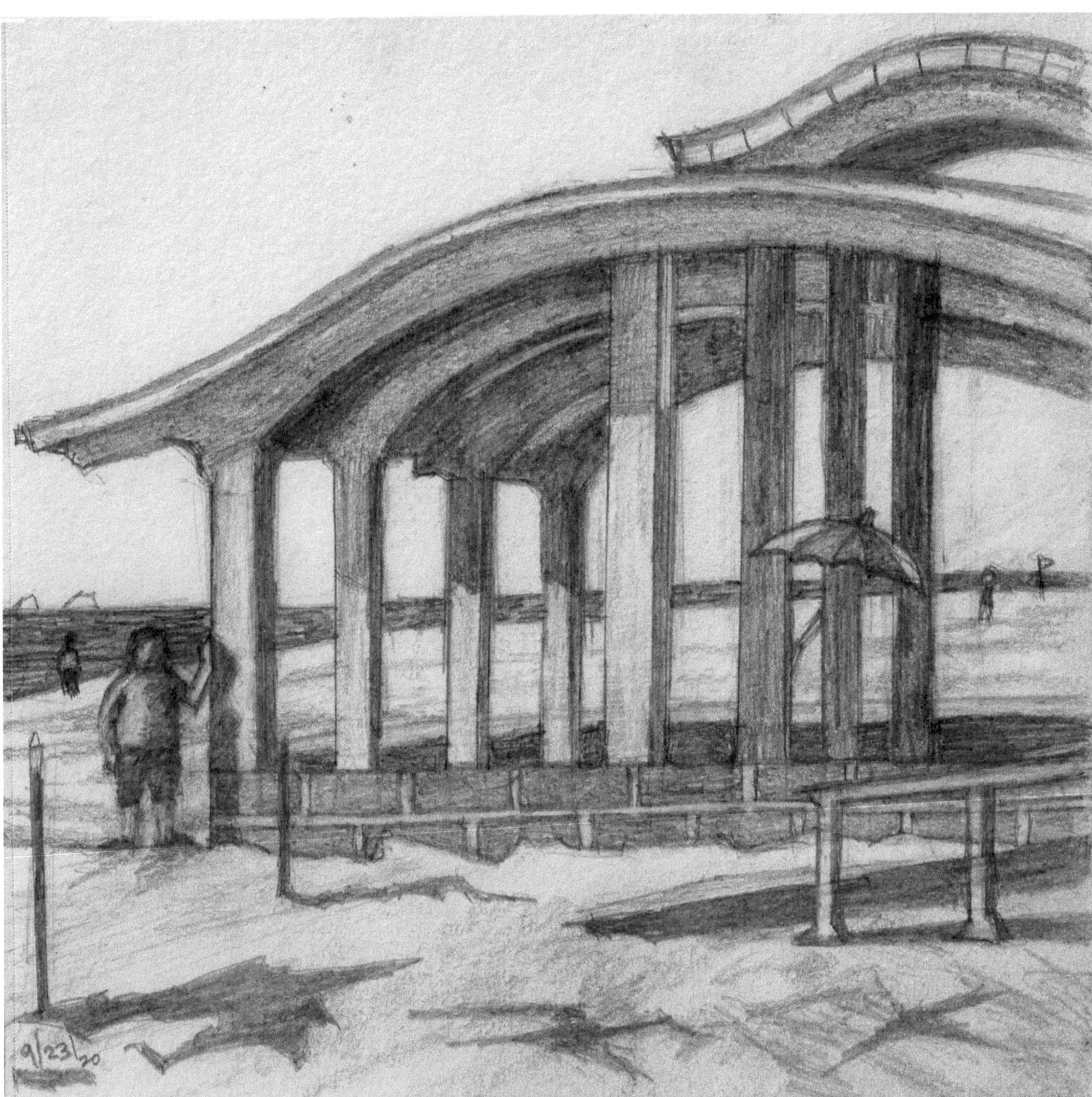
9/23/20

Luna Games

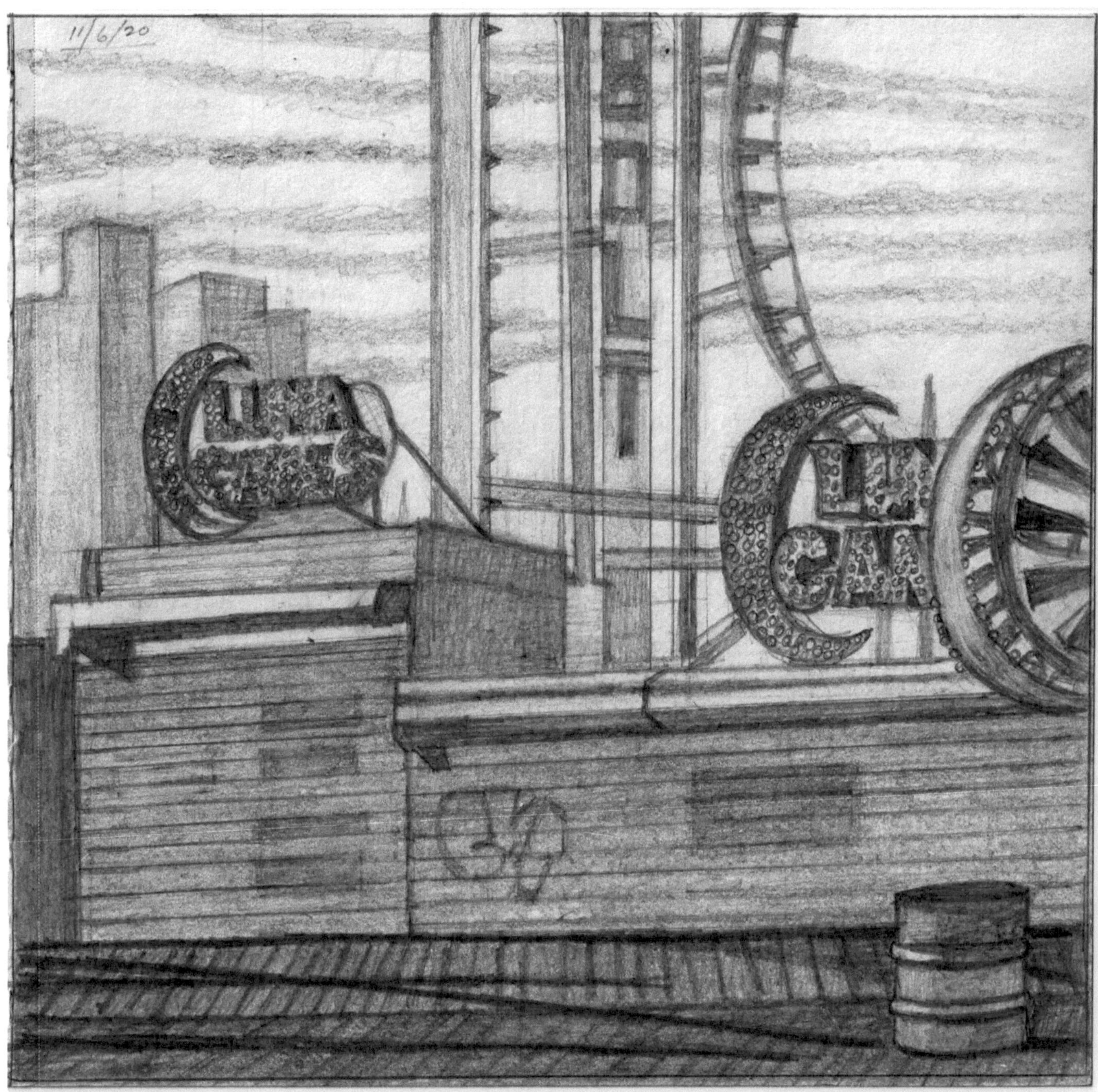

11/6/20
LUNA
PARK

Carousel

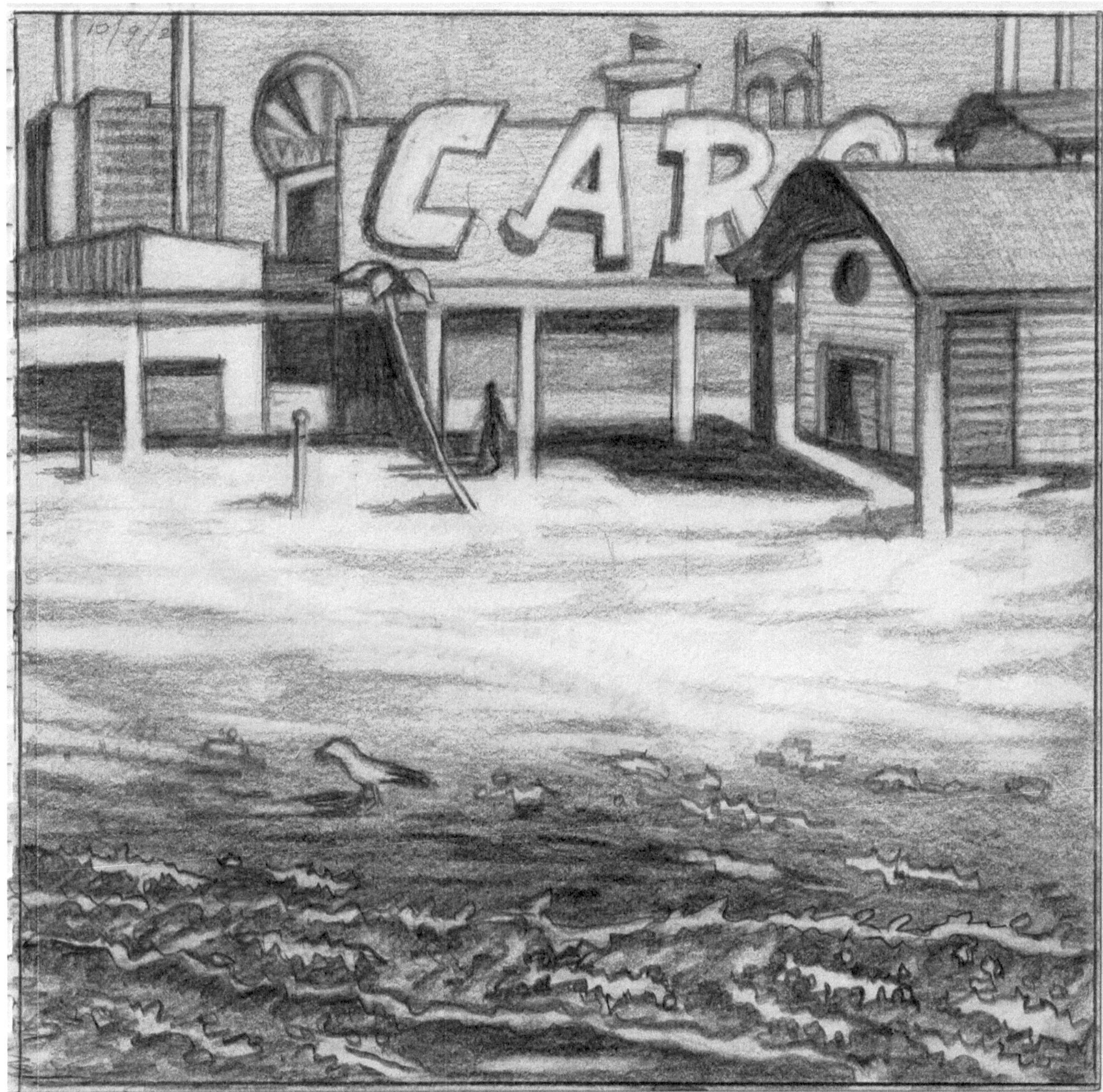

CARS

Ticket Booth

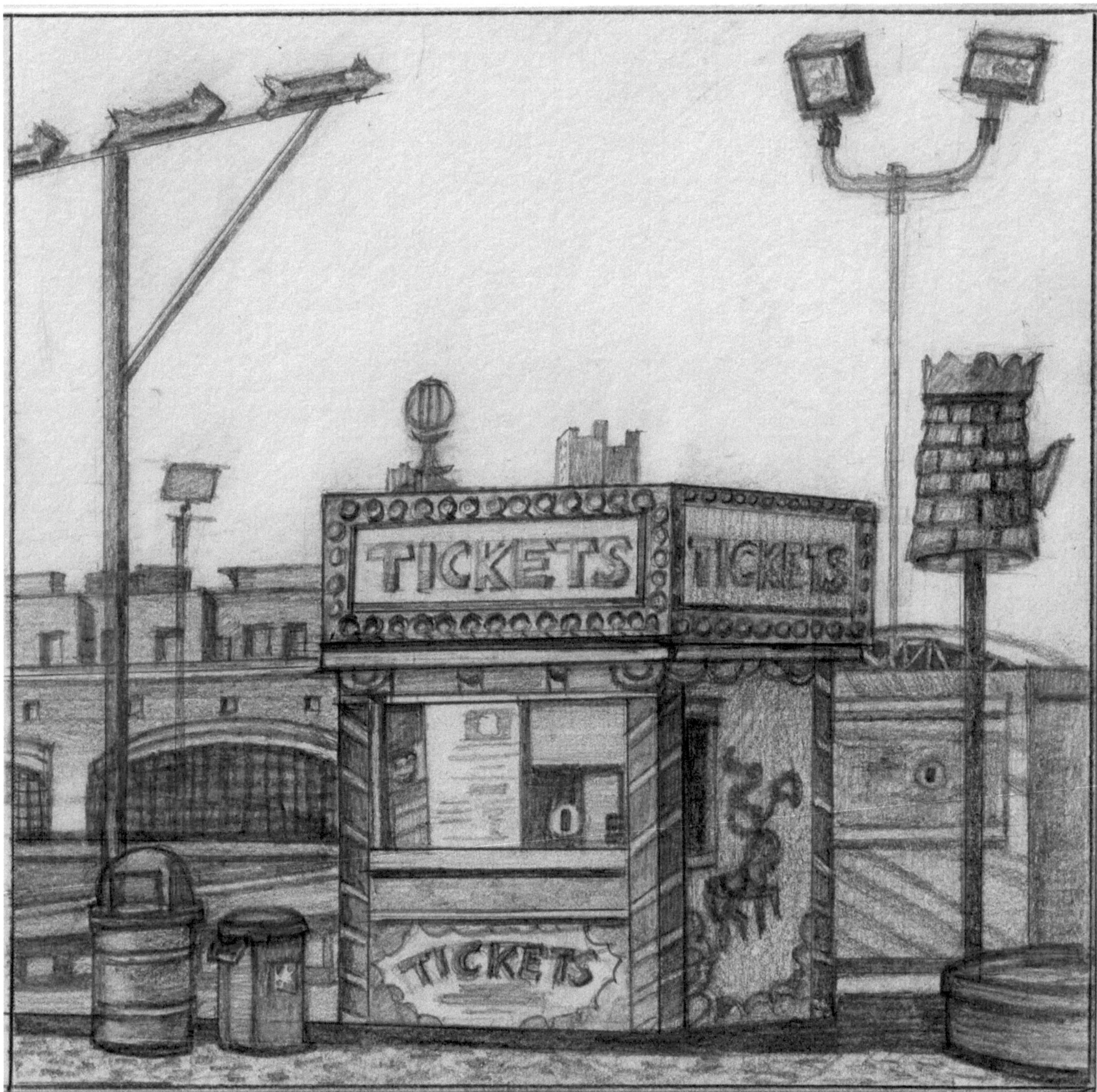

TICKETS
TICKETS
TICKETS

Coney Island Gothic

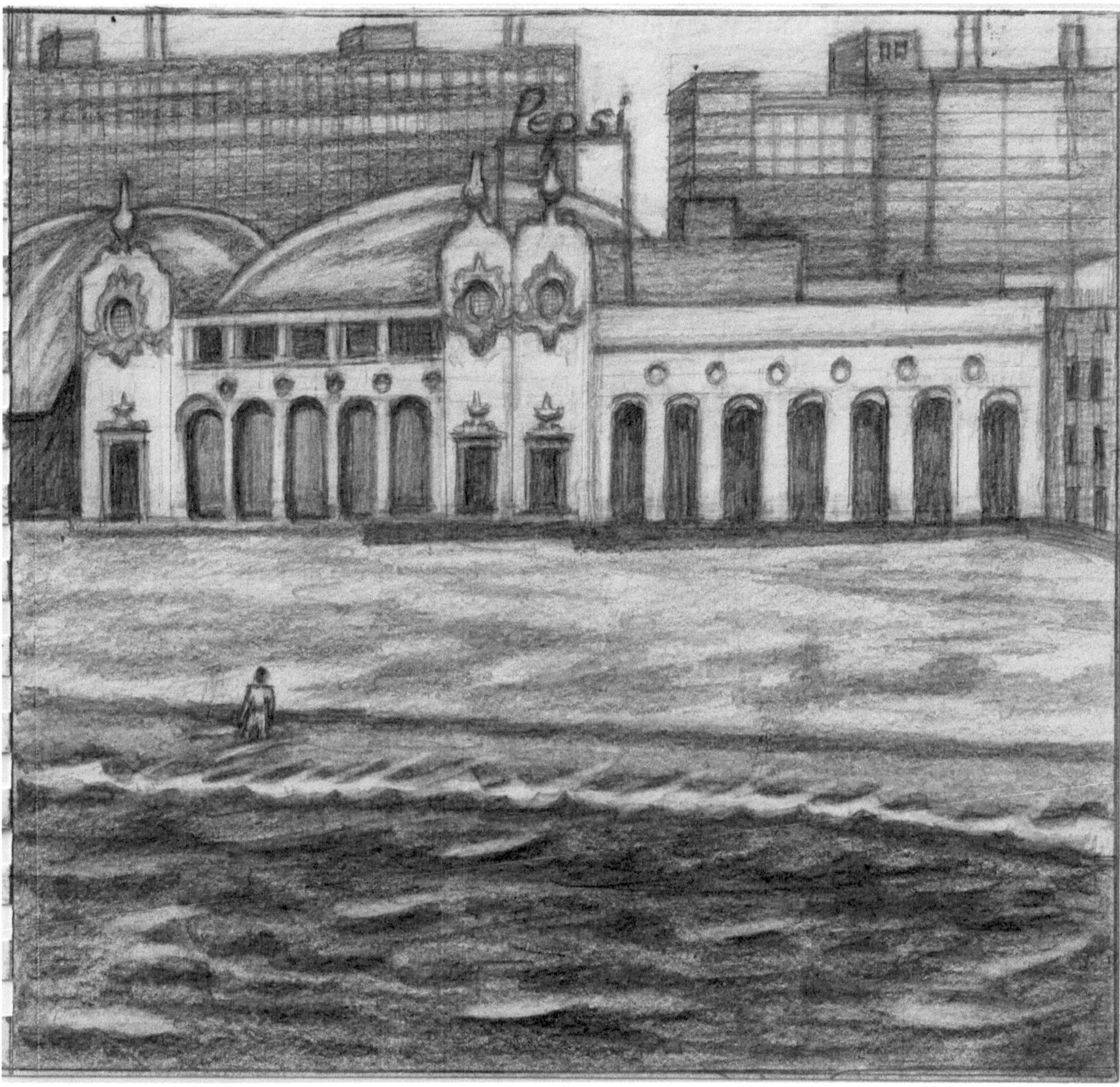

Pepsi

Coney Island Wagons

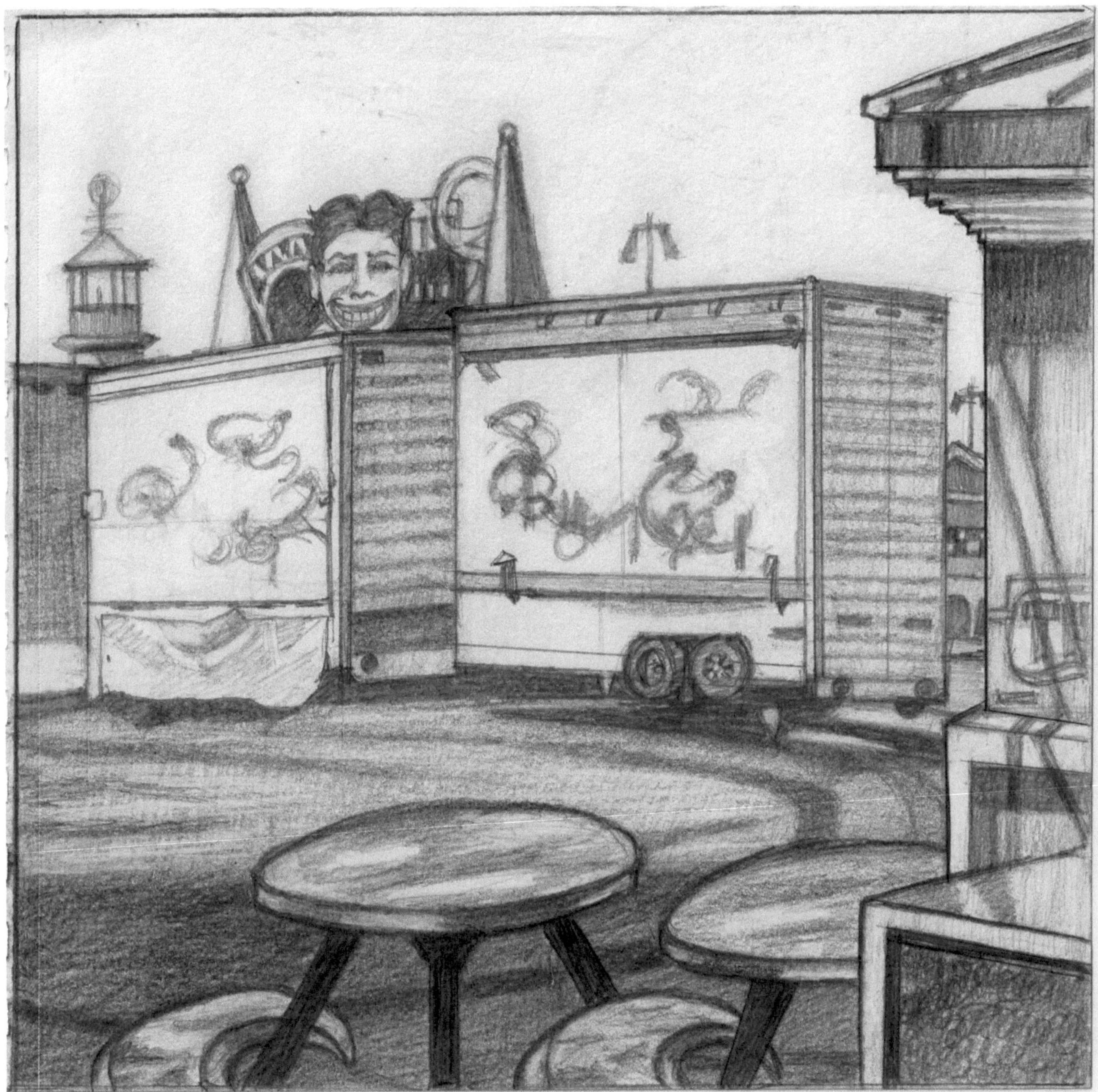

Arches and Shadows

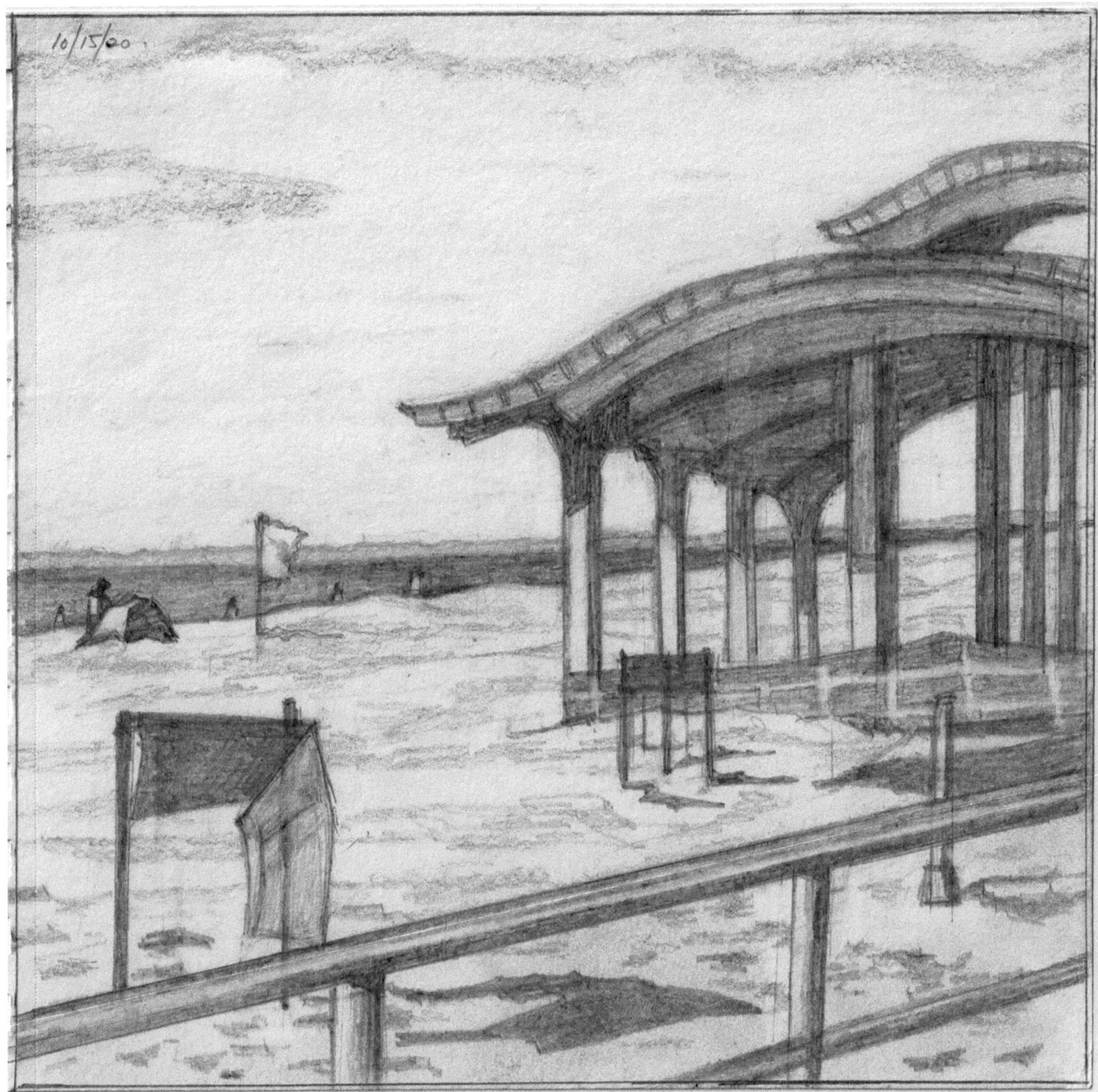
10/15/20

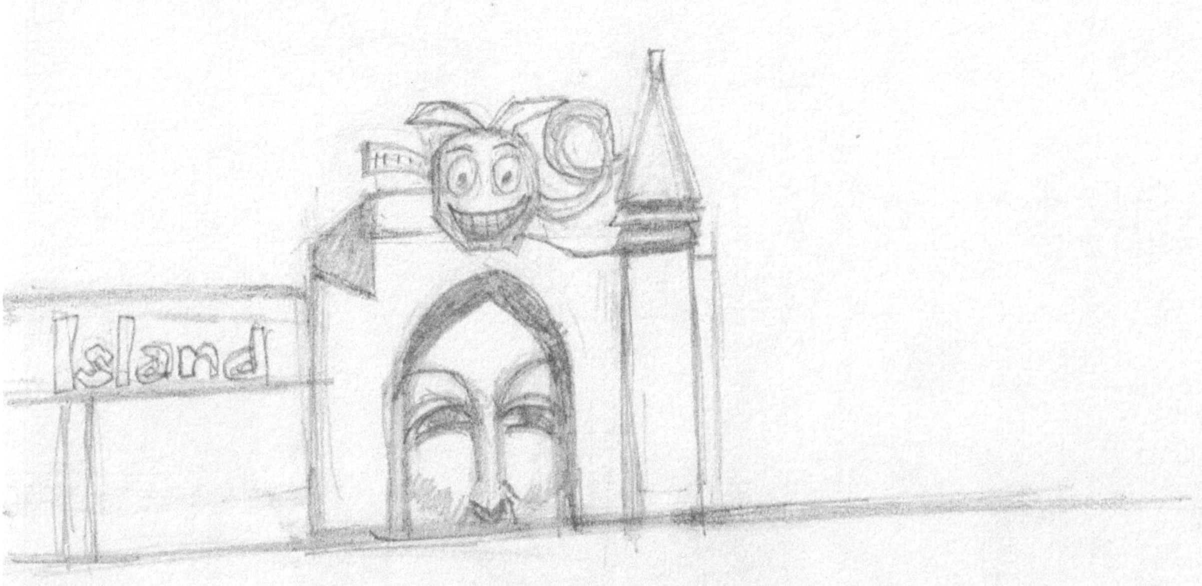

Sketchbook

Bright
yellow-
orange
↓

blue   red   pale
  green   orange   lime

8/21/20

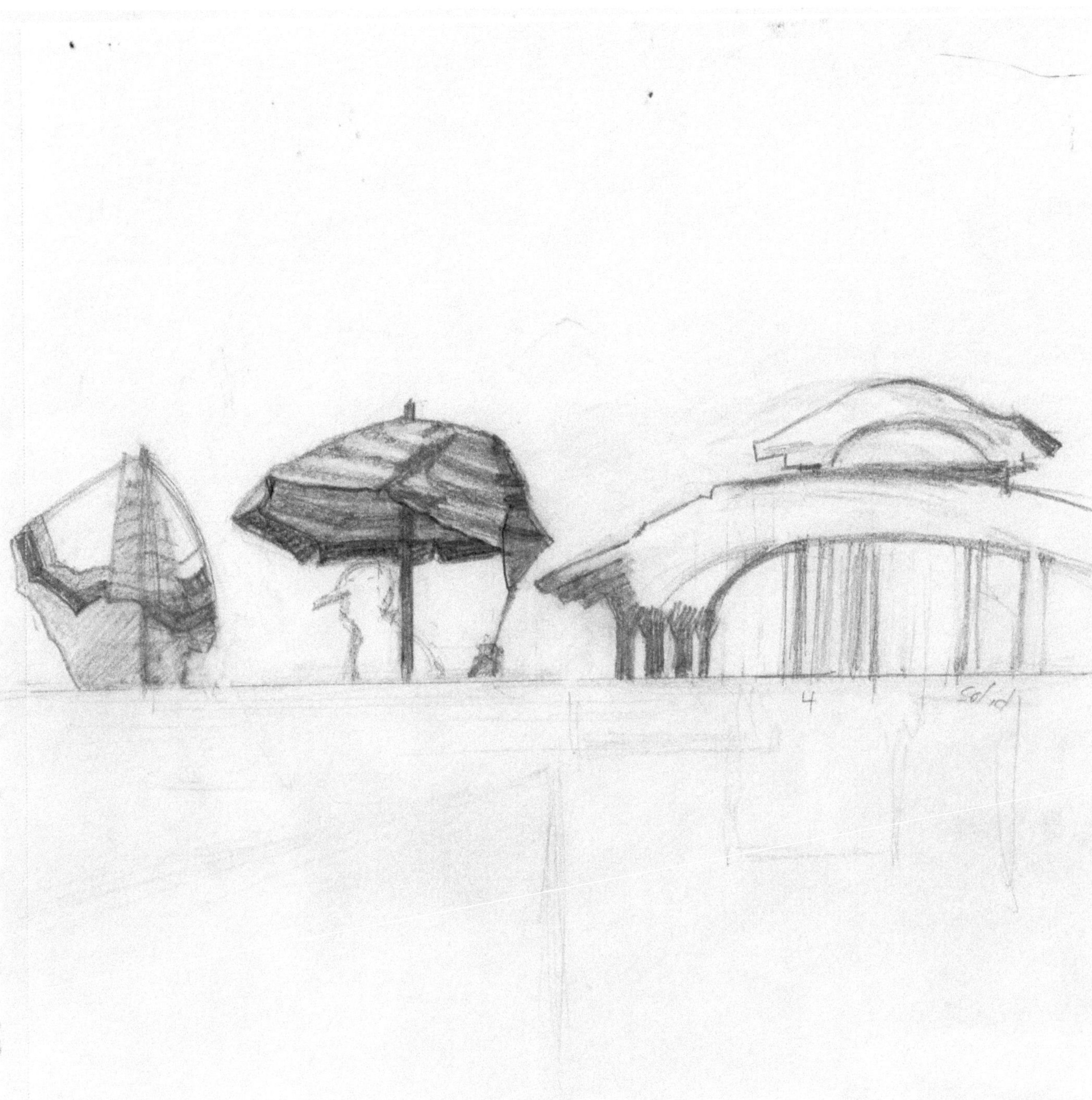

4
solid

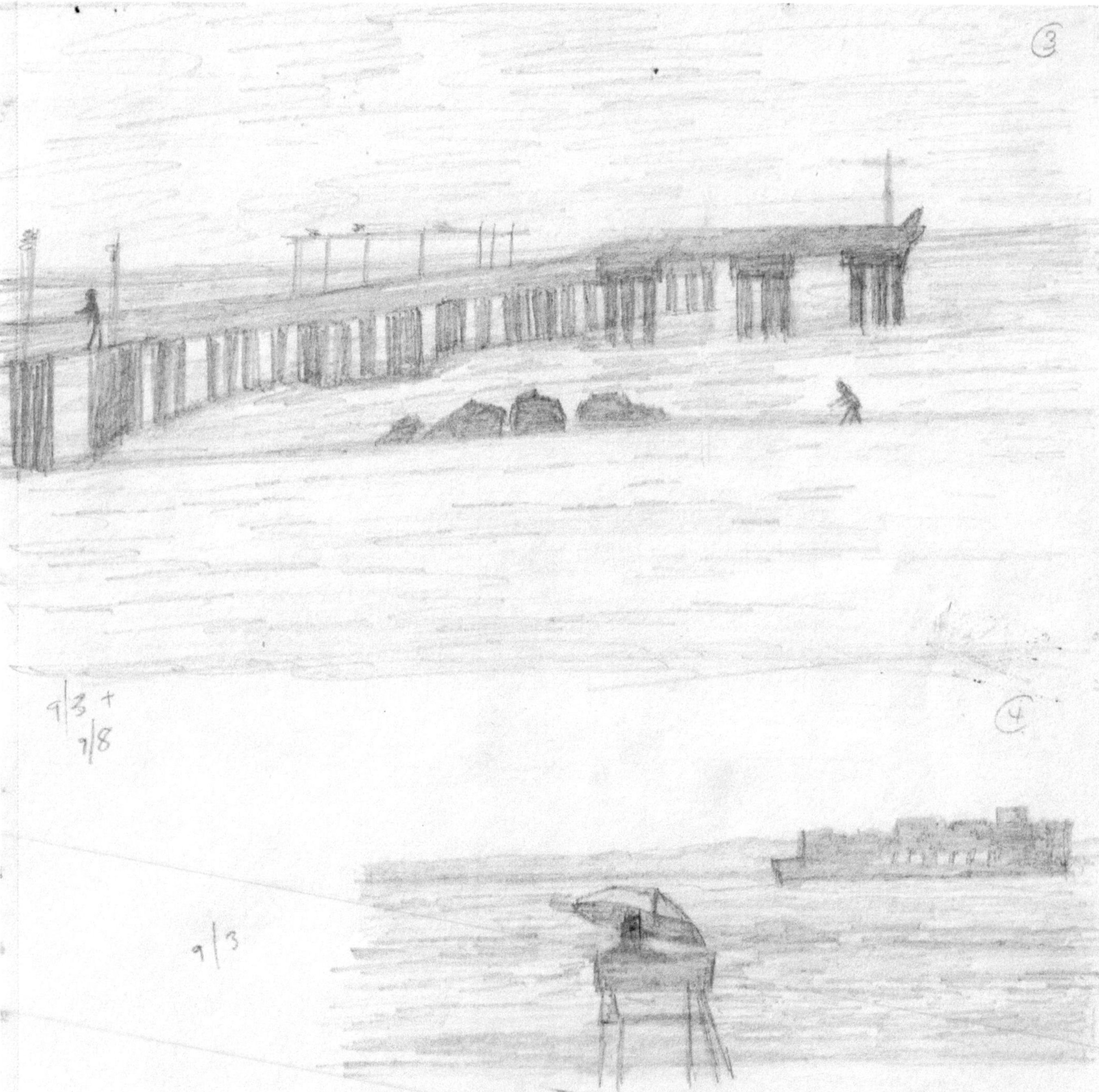
3
9/3 +
7/8
9/3
4

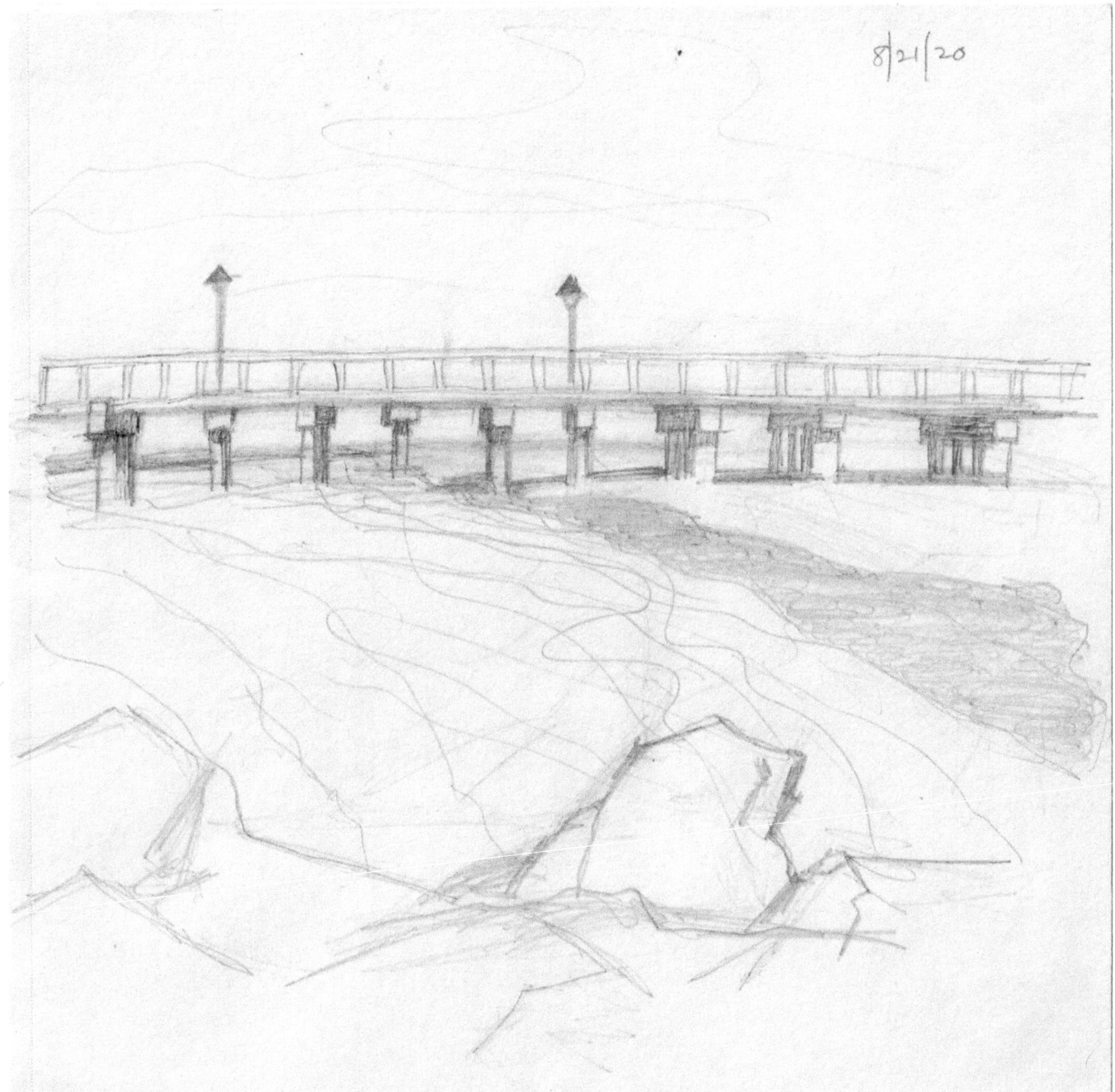
8/21/20

This looks
like Fouquet's
"Devils
leaving
Paris".

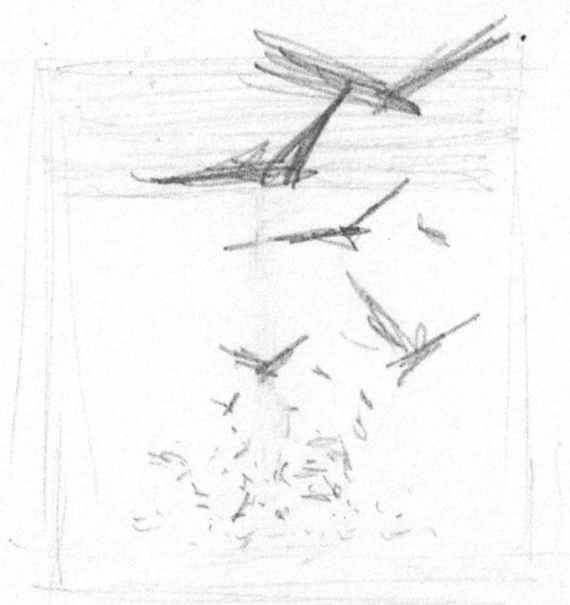

seagulls being
fed

8/29 this new work —
the theme of this new work is people, or
figures, in relation to the ocean + the
boardwalk

pale blue
← blue purple
← blue grey
☐ blue green

9/3/20

②

I like the lone
figure in
these
drawings.

10/14/20